King of the Shattered Glass

By Susan Joy Bellavance

For my Goddaughter.
Love, Uncle Mike
Christmas 2022

Illustrations by Sara Tang

Available from:
Marian Helpers Center
Stockbridge, MA 01263
1-800-462-7426
marian.org
ShopMercy.org

ISBN: 978-1-59614-398-2

Nihil Obstat:
Dr. Robert A. Stackpole, STD
Censor Deputatus
May 1, 2017

This book is printed with soy-based ink.

Printed in the United States of America

MARIAN PRESS
STOCKBRIDGE MA 01263

Susan Bellavance served with the Missionaries of Charity, was a Catholic elementary and junior high school teacher, and founding member of Mount Royal Academy, in Sunapee, New Hampshire. She also served as a catechist and as a youth group leader. In addition to writing, Susan is a Marian Helper who currently volunteers at Bishop Peterson Residence, a home for retired and elderly priests in the Diocese of Manchester. She resides with her cherished husband, Dale, and two treasured daughters, Sophia and Marguerite, in New Hampshire.

Dedication

To my dear husband, Dale, and our daughters, Sophia and Marguerite;
to Deb Mckew, Mother of Writers;
and to our beloved priests, images of the Father's tenderness
in the Sacrament of His Mercy.

– SJB

For my family, friends, and those most in need of the healing,
life-giving power of Love and Mercy.

– SMT

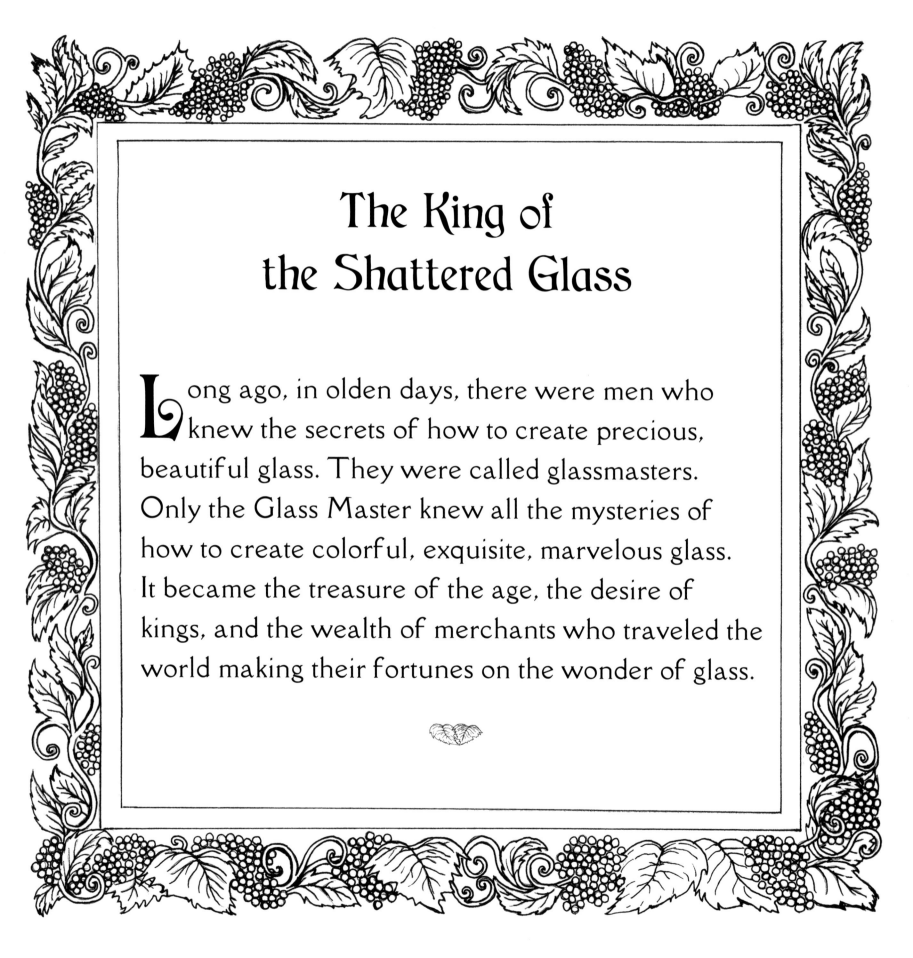

The King of the Shattered Glass

Long ago, in olden days, there were men who knew the secrets of how to create precious, beautiful glass. They were called glassmasters. Only the Glass Master knew all the mysteries of how to create colorful, exquisite, marvelous glass. It became the treasure of the age, the desire of kings, and the wealth of merchants who traveled the world making their fortunes on the wonder of glass.

Little Marguerite tied her apron as she hurried down the long, winding stairwell. "I'm late, I'm late, I'm late! I hope Master Chef doesn't find out!" She sped across the stone floor of the castle kitchen. And what a kitchen! Cooks prepared wonderful food for hordes of guests, soldiers, servants, and, of course, the King.

Marguerite hurried to light the oven fires and fetch the water before Master Chef arrived.

When she rushed to grab the water buckets hanging by the back door, she collided with stout Master Chef Louis coming in from the gardens.

"If you are late in the morning," he boiled, "then the baker is late, then the bread is late, then the breakfast is late, and then the King is late!"

"I promise to work faster, Master Chef, you will see," said Marguerite with her sweetest smile.

"*Mon Dieu!* Give me patience!" prayed Master Chef heavenward. He only pretended to be angry, because with the orphan Marguerite, he was like butter in a pan.

A delicious rumor spilled through the castle kitchen. Olivero the Merchant was coming from far away, and his cart was filled with unknown treasures.

"Perhaps he brings spices to improve the soup," joked Master Chef.

"Bah," said the Soup Cook with a splash of his spoon.

The thundering clank of the drawbridge excited Marguerite. She ran to the Great Hall and hid behind a large chair to sneak a glimpse of the treasure.

"Gently, gently!" said Master Olivero to the servants who carried the crates into the hall. When the King entered, Marguerite thought how tall and noble he looked. It

was said that no one could hold his gaze for long, for his eyes searched and pierced the heart.

Olivero carefully pulled something out of the straw-filled boxes. Candlelight sparkled on it.

"What is it?"

"It's called glass, Sire."

"Glass," the King repeated.

He had never beheld such a thing. From the crates appeared goblets and bowls of every size, some as blue as the Aegean Sea, others the color of midsummer honey. He held an amber bowl to the candle on the table. The flame danced right through it.

"So transparent, so exquisite," said the King. "How is it made?"

"Ah, that is a secret known only to the glassmakers."

The King's sleeve brushed against a goblet, and it crashed to the floor, shattering into pieces. "So beautiful, and so brittle," said the King. "But now I see; I must not only have the glass; I must have the glassmaker!"

"Glass is the new wealth of the age, Majesty. But glassmakers are almost impossible to come by, unless ..."

"Unless?" inquired the King.

"Unless you are Olivero the Merchant," he said with a bow.

Months passed, and, true to his word, Olivero brought a wise old glassmaster to the King. The Glass Master brought his tools, his craft secrets, and his very pesky young son, Giovanni.

A special courtyard and a glassmaker's furnace were built. Guards were posted to keep intruders and the curious away. Only the Glass Master's men were allowed entry. Smoke billowed day and night as the Glass Master began to create a magnificent collection fit for a king.

Soon glass began to fill the kitchen shelves, followed by a decree from the King: Anyone who broke the King's glass was to bring the pieces to him.

But, what would happen if the King's glass was broken? No one wanted to find out.

One terrible day, Marguerite balanced on a stool to empty her buckets into the washtub, when the back door silently opened. It was that rascal Giovanni again, sneaking into the kitchen to steal a fresh, crusty loaf of bread.

"Marguerite!" yelled the Baker. "It's Giovanni! Get the broom!"

Startled, Marguerite overturned the stool. Water splashed everywhere. She could not reach the broom in time!

"Giovanni, you thief!" scolded Marguerite. "You put that back!"

He took a big bite and grinned at her. With a wiggle of his derriere and wave of his hand, Giovanni dashed for the door.

Marguerite's anger blazed. She grabbed the first object that was not bolted down, the King's crimson goblet, and hurled it at Giovanni. In astonished horror she watched it fly through the air. Giovanni cleared the doorway with a leap and a laugh. The goblet smashed into pieces against the slamming door.

"Oh, no!" said the Baker.

"Oh, no!" said Master Chef.

"Oh, no!" said Marguerite. She had shattered the King's glass.

Marguerite bent down to gather the shards in her apron.

Master Chef whispered in her ear, "Give those to me. The King will never know. You will be punished!"

"How do you know?" asked Marguerite innocently.

"Well, we don't know *exactly* what will happen," interrupted the Baker.
"No one has ever brought broken glass to the King. We have all hid it or buried it somewhere."

"I must go," said Marguerite to the panicked Master Chef. "I want to go."

Down the long, long corridor to the King's court she went.

"The scullion Marguerite," announced the Bailiff, opening the heavy arched door. When Marguerite beheld the King's majestic appearance as he sat upon his throne, her heart pounded and her knees weakened. She froze. Even when he beckoned her, Marguerite was unable to move. Seeing this, the King arose, removed his gold crown, and went to her.

"Why have you come?" the King inquired tenderly.

"I ... I ... ," she stuttered. "I have come on the occasion of shattered glass." Opening her apron, she revealed the shards of the King's favorite goblet. Removing the red sash that crossed his chest, the King bent low and held it open beneath Marguerite's apron.

"Give everything to me," he said.

She placed each broken piece into his sash. Gently laying his hand upon her head, he said, "I forgive you. You may go." His kindness moved Marguerite's heart more than any punishment could. Tears trickled down her cheeks. She turned and walked to the door.

The Bailiff assumed she was punished. "After all, His Majesty is always just," he thought to himself.

When Marguerite told all to Master Chef, he stubbornly held to his fears of punishment. "Something will come of this, I tell you," he warned, raising his caterpillar eyebrows so high in disbelief they almost touched his cooking cap.

Some days later, while Marguerite emptied ashes behind the kitchen, Giovanni strolled by. "Get out of here, you bread thief!"

"I have decided we should be friends. I'm going to tell you a secret."

"What secret?" asked Marguerite suspiciously.

"A secret that no one else in the whole kingdom knows. A secret I can't even tell you. I have to *show* you!" He grabbed her hand and ran with her to the Glass Master's courtyard. When the guard wasn't looking, they crept through the forbidden doors and hid behind some sacks of sand. A furnace, shaped like a giant beehive, rumbled and roared with fire while workers and craftsmen swarmed all about.

"This is the secret," whispered Giovanni. "See, they mix sand and ashes and then put them in the hot furnace, and it melts them like wax."

"What's he doing now?" asked Marguerite, seeing the Glass Master open the tiny furnace door.

"He gathers the melted sand at the end of that long pipe and blows into it."

"Ah!" whispered Marguerite. The molten stuff blew into a big fiery ball. The Glass Master kept spinning the pipe to keep the ball from collapsing. "What will it become?"

"A bowl, a goblet, a flying bird — whatever the Glass Master wishes it to be." It was pure magic. Suddenly, a worker approached their hiding place. Giovanni grabbed Marguerite's hand and they ran back across the field.

"That's a secret my father taught me," bragged Giovanni breathlessly arriving at the kitchen. "Now it's your turn to tell a secret!" The orphan Marguerite thought hard for a moment.

"My father taught me the art of juggling," she said, cherishing his memory.

"You lie. No one teaches that to girls," goaded Giovanni.

"Well, my father did, and I can juggle anything at all. Anything!"

Then Giovanni sprang his trap. "Can you juggle glass?"

"Of course, anything," she said. *Did he say glass?*

"Then show me how clever your father really was by juggling the King's glass."

They stole into the pantry. Rows of the King's glass filled the shelves.

"These," said Giovanni, pointing. "Juggle these bowls, and you will prove that your father was a clever man. Refuse, and you will agree with me that he was a fool."

Marguerite was indignant. She picked up the bowls one by one and tossed them into the air. Suddenly, in walked Master Chef.

"*Sacré Bleu!* Marguerite!" he cried. "What are you doing?"

Crash! Crash! Crash! Crash! Crash! Giovanni ran like a frightened weasel.

"Oh, no! I did this! He said my father was ... ." The tears began. "Why do I care what that boy says about my father?"

When Master Chef saw Marguerite bending down to hold open her apron, he objected.

"No, Marguerite, don't! You cannot take them to the King again! I will take care of this."

But Marguerite had already collected half of the broken pieces.

"You know, Monsieur, you already know ... ."

Master Chef held the door and his tongue. Marguerite was brokenhearted, but she knew where she must go.

"How will he forgive me for doing this again?" Marguerite thought. But, when the King saw Marguerite approach him with her bulging apron, he marveled at her courage.

"Were you hurt?"

"Not on the outside, Sire."

"Tell me," said the King.

"He mocked my father." Pent-up sobs escaped from her very heart.

"Who did?"

"Giovanni, the glassmaker's boy."

"Hmmm ... I see. So you had to defend your father's honor with my glass?" asked the King softly.

"Giovanni said that if I didn't juggle the glass, I would prove that my father was a fool. I was wrong to listen to him. I am very sorry for what I have done," she said with her tear-stained face upturned.

The King's heart was moved with compassion. Gently, he placed his hands on either side of Marguerite's face and gazed into her eyes. His were the kindest eyes she had ever seen. His gaze penetrated her heart. For all the glass she had broken, his kindheartedness was almost unbearable.

"I forgive you," he said. "But you must do something for me."

"Whatever you ask, Your Highness."

"When you are done with your regular duties ... "

"Yes?"

"Go and help Giovanni with his, for one week."

"Oh! But ... Oh, my." Marguerite's face flushed. "Yes, Your Majesty, I promise."

For love of you, my gentle King, thought Marguerite, but it will be so hard!

The King removed his sash and held it open for Marguerite. The shards tumbled from her apron, down to the last colored splinter.

For the next week, Giovanni the teaser could not understand why Marguerite was so kind to him. She kept her promise to the King at all costs. At the end of the sacrifice, something unexpected happened: Giovanni began to change.

It was the Feast of St. John the Baptist, and the castle kitchen buzzed with preparations. "Minstrels! Music! Jugglers!" Marguerite swirled a little dance with her broom.

"Master Chef, about tonight. I thought that if I were to stop my work to hear the minstrels tell their story, and then afterwards ..."

"Marguerite," Master Chef interrupted, "we are the servants of the King, not his dinner guests! Tonight, every duke and earl will be here to see the King's magnificent glass laid out at the banquet. You know what that means!"

"But why can't I finish my duties after the performances?" Marguerite begged.

"Ah, no! Duty first, amusement after — everything else spells disaster. Oh, I like the sound of that," said Master Chef as he waddled away.

The faster Marguerite worked, the more water spilled and splashed. Soon, the sound of the Minstrel's lute drifted into the kitchen. Marguerite could stand it no longer! She stacked dishes very high to make just one trip to the glass pantry. Slide went her feet, slip went her hands, and smash went the plates, bowls, and platters!

Marguerite surveyed the mountain of broken glass before her. Remembering the kind eyes of the King, she cried, "This is all my fault! How will I face him again?" Marguerite wept into her apron. "I will tell him it was an accident," she said. Deep down, she knew it was her desire to please herself that was the real cause.

"How will he know that I love him when he sees all this?"

It wasn't the shattered glass that had made Marguerite cry; it was her broken heart.

This time, it was Master Chef's huge apron that she filled. Struggling, she pulled the apron behind her down the corridor. If I go to the throne room now, I can wait there until morning and see the King before anyone else sees me, she thought. Down the long corridor she dragged her bundle, past servants and guards jamming the doorway of the Great Hall, their attention riveted on the minstrel and his wonderful tale.

There were candles still lit in the throne room. Surely the servants will be back before the night is over, she thought.

"I must hide somewhere where they won't see me and send me away," she whispered to herself, looking about. "There," she said. "I will hide behind the throne. No one will look up there."

She hid behind his throne and sobbed herself to sleep on the floor. Late that night, the King returned with pressing work to do.

"What is this?" he asked. Something was sticking out from behind his throne. The guard sprang upon the steps.

"It's that kitchen waif again," said the guard. "Shall I remove her, your Majesty?"

"Where does she stay?" asked the King.

"In the high turret," replied the guard.

The King bent down and pushed the hair from Marguerite's tear-stained face.

Hard work and grief had made her insensible to the sounds around her. He saw the bundle of shattered glass at the girl's side and shook his head.

"Marguerite, Marguerite, whatever shall I do with you?" smiled the King.

Lifting her in his arms, he followed the guard up the winding stairs to the place where her pallet of straw lay. Gently leaning down, he placed her on her bed and covered her with her small blanket. "Your heart is true, little one," he whispered, touching her forehead with his fingertips. "You are more precious than glass to me." Her humble honesty had won his heart.

Marguerite slept soundly until the morning sunshine awakened her. Confused, she quickly wrestled to her feet. Turning about, she looked for her bundle of shattered glass. It was gone. "What ... how ... ?" She stood silent with her hands on each side of her head for a moment, trying to remember the night before, when suddenly the Lauds bell rang.

"Oh, no!" she cried. Off to the kitchen she ran.

"Marguerite! You are late," said Master Chef. "But I will forgive you this time. I couldn't see where you were standing when the minstrel told his tale. Did you make it in time?"

Before she could answer, Master Chef trundled off. Everyone in the kitchen knew that there was glass missing, but no one wanted Marguerite to go back to the King.

Every year when the leaves were turning gold, on the Feast of Michaelmas, the entire Kingdom, nobles and peasants alike, gathered for a celebration. This year, the King invited everyone to a special banquet in the Great Hall for the unveiling of a tremendous surprise.

When Michaelmas arrived, the castle kitchen burst with commotion long before the sun awoke. Roasting meats hissed and popped on slowly turned spits; cauldrons bubbled with stews and gravies. Everywhere there was a scent or a sizzle.

Marguerite fetched and carried, but all the while, in her heart, she pictured the King's face. How thrilling it was that the King had commanded even the kitchen staff to join in the banquet! In fact, they were instructed to sit at the King's table! The Angelus bells signaled everyone to take their places. The kitchen staff felt awkward sitting at the King's high table; Marguerite the scullery maid was utterly bewildered — her seat was next to the King's!

The King arrived to a thunderous welcome. "Today you will all be privileged to see something that has never been seen in this Kingdom before!" He signaled to the servants. One by one they pulled back huge drapes to reveal immense glass windows. Sunshine burst in through the panes.

"Beautiful!" "Glorious!" "Amazing!" Applause filled the hall.

Finally, the King stood beneath the last curtain, and looked in Marguerite's direction. He signaled for silence. Marguerite's heart began to pound.

"Virtue of the heart is its own reward," said the King, "but, virtue towards the King deserves the King's reward."

He pulled back the drapes. Dazzling light revealed an image of the King placing a crown on a young girl holding open her apron. The window was fashioned out of all the shattered pieces of glass Marguerite had brought to the King.

Giovanni jumped up on his bench and shouted, "It's Marguerite, the scullery maid!"

"Marguerite," said the King in his gentle voice, "I would like you to become my daughter."

"What?!" exclaimed Master Chef.

The King had barely finished the words when Marguerite flew from her place at the table and into the King's open arms.

"I love you!" she cried.

"My princess," he said, as she sobbed for joy, "my princess."

The King carried Marguerite to her place next to him. She looked up with shining eyes at the King, her new father.

"I will never bury my broken glass again," remarked Master Chef, winking to the Baker.

All the people, even Giovanni, cheered.

The End